619

Thank you to everyone who provided their time
and constructive criticism on this project.
You are all greatly appreciated.

LAF

LOSTARTFILE LLC

LOSTARTFILE, LLC

Dover, Delaware

Cover Design: Gencie

Publishing Consultant: Sedrik Newbern, Newbern Consulting, LLC

Editor: Linda Shew Wolf, Network Publishing Partners, Inc.

Printed in the United States of America
First Edition: June 2025

ISBN Paperback: 979-8-218-70541-1

Library of Congress Control Number: 2025911749

This book was written as it was intended to be.
The format and contents of this book were
meticulously and strategically chosen per the
author's artistic expression.
The traditional expectations of formality and
consistency are constantly challenged throughout
the book to incite and invoke a sense of change
within the reader.

TABLE OF CONTENTS

SECTION 1

What Are You Reading This For?

What are you reading this for?
To evoke some sort of emotion?
To analyze the words of others?
To compare?
To scrutinize?
Or is it for inspiration?
Or is it because you're bored?
Why are you reading this?
What are you trying to get out of it?
What will it do for you?
What will you do with it?
Are you trying to give it meaning?
Did you expect this?
Is this what you wanted?

A Poem

This poem could be better
But it has many flaws
It tries and tries and tries
But it fails to no avail

This poem is a work in progress
Even though it is complete
In some areas it is strong
In some areas it is weak

This poem is what it is
It will never be what it is not
This is a poem about itself
This is all the poem has got

Like the poem
Hate the poem
Think it is good
Think it is bad

It is
In the end
A poem

What Is Poetry?

Poetry is…
A voice for the ones who are not heard
A weapon for the ones who are defenseless
A dream for all those who are restless
A medicine for those who are wounded

Poetry is…
A truth that is used to dispel falsehoods
A solution that is given to solve problems
A statement that challenges preconceived notions

Poetry is…
A manifestation of one's imagination
An epiphany of the complexities of reality
An expression of unadulterated emotions
A thought-provoking stimulant waiting to be interpreted

Art

Believe me I know how vulnerable it can be

Having to express your feelings and emotions

Coupled with sharing your inner thoughts and possible insecurities

That's why I love it

Because of the raw expression

A side of yourself you might not otherwise show

Forcing yourself to feel comfortable with opening up

Sharing your views with all who are receptive to receiving

Accepting any possible judgment or criticism

Embracing it for all of what it is

There's true beauty in the process of creation

The allure of sharing your finished product

It's something to live for

Let Us Think

As long as we are alive we are in a constant state of thought
We think when we're awake, we think when we're asleep
Thinking is inevitable
Even when we try not to think about anything
We are still thinking about not thinking
So since we are forced to think, let us think consciously
Let us think theoretically, rooted in the abstract
Let us think pragmatically, rooted in logic
Let us think about the past thoughts once thought
Let us think about all the thoughts that have yet to be thought
Let us think for as long as we can think
Let us think about whatever we want to think about
And may we never stop thinking about things that make us think

Why

Why do we live?
Why do we die?
Why do we dream?
Why do we wonder why?

Why do we do anything at all?

SECTION 2

Prisoners of Existence

We are prisoners of existence being forced to serve life
The essence of being encapsulated into a mere moment in time
Constantly constructing a reality out of a sense of perception
The absence of death fueling the notion of life
Immersed in the possibility of understanding the unknown
Experiences limited through the condition of one's sense of self
Freed only by the death of our very own existence

Duality of Man

Too much yin for the yang
Too much yang for the yin
Filled with righteousness
Overflowing with sin
He's a demon seed
But he's heaven sent
Sadistic in nature
But yet so benevolent
Since his conception
The struggle began
The fight to understand
The duality of man

Reality

I had a dream
Or maybe it was a nightmare
I was in the future
Or maybe it was the past
Now that I think about it
I'm not so sure I was asleep at all

Time

Some say time is like a line
The past, the present and the future
Some say time is like a circle
A cycle that constantly repeats itself
I say time is like a spiral
Expanding with the possibilities chosen

The Beauty of Life

The beauty of life is encapsulated into moments
Moments frozen in time
Sketched into the brain
Forging memories to last the length of a lifetime

SECTION 3

I'm a Psychedelic Psychopath

I'm a psychedelic psychopath

A mushroom addict

A marijuana fanatic

It's magnanimously magnificent, for all of you that's missing it

So majestic when you ingest it

Prolific, profound, prophetic, profane

It's insane, the power of the brain

The conception of perception is a mere reflection of your inner affections

No incarceration on my imagination

Spewing out wild lamentations with no consideration of implications

Nothing is what it seems

Reality is a mere dream

Don't get caught up in the scheme

Do you mind if I free your mind like I freed mine

It's trapped in a box like a mime

Waiting for a chance to escape the fate that waits for nobody

Not even time

Immediate, expedient, obedient

Satirical, spiritual, hysterical

Confusion and delusion

This society is a miracle

It's like a paradox in which you ponder and pontificate

No need to deliberate

Karma is what you reciprocate

It's only a matter of time before we are all awake

The 3 W's

Wild
Are the ones that do not know
>The misguided
>The unaware
>The oblivious

Wicked
Are the ones who know but choose to do the opposite
>The deceiver
>The misleader
>The pretender

Wise
Are the ones who know and act on what they know
>The guide
>The leader
>The teacher

False Oaths

R.I.P. to all the dead
Eye for an eye
That's what it said
Stick the needle in the thread
Poke the skin
Then it bled
Drink the blood
Eat the bread
Get on your knees
Bow your head
Put your hand over your heart
Now say a pledge
For the money and for the life
Mark upon the forehead

Sitting by a Pond

You can catch me sitting by a pond surrounded by ponderosas watching pondfish while ponderating about the ponderings of life

Enlightenment

I'm like a thief in the night
A Robin Hood of sorts
I'm here to steal your ignorance
And bring forth the light
Expanding your consciousness
Blinding you with the influx of information
Transforming your energy
Sending waves straight into your third eye
Penetrating deep into your inner essence
The sense of what is beyond the senses
The knowledge of self
Discovered only by discovering the knowledge of the universe

Ignorance Is Bliss

Ignorance is bliss
And knowledge is a burden to bear
The loss of ignorance is misery and pain
That's why knowledge is a scary thing to gain

Can we talk?

Let's indulge in a conscious cognitive conversation.
Gratifying while simultaneously captivating.
It's stimulating.
No debating the eloquent articulation.
The combination of emotion mixed with passion.
That's what I'm anticipating.
Can I pick your brain while you pick mine?
Particularly the parts that interest me.
I inquire, I inquest.
Heavily invest.
Full concentration, content with deep consideration.
Unadulterated, unequivocal motivation.
So vivacious, so voracious.
Can you face this?
Can you taste bliss?
No patience.
It's an opportunity I can't miss!

Can we talk?

Slang

Please excuse my dialectic vernacular
The verbiage in which I use to speak
It is so enriched, far superior, beyond weak
The prestige of my preferred speech
Can you dig the profound prodigious perplexities
My ebonic idiolect is so perfect
Peculiarities of my speech make you stare at me
It's pathetic that you don't understand
The prophetic words of a man
No need to be rude
My language is often misconstrued
They say it's improper
That I'm speaking incorrect
All I say is, "fasho" and "aight bet"
You do you
And I'll do me
And we'll be just fine
I'll never abandon this language of mine

SECTION 4

It Is What It Is Where I'm From

It is what it is where I'm from
Until it's not
Things change
Dreams fade
And life becomes a memory

Death Note

I saw her coming
I did not try to fight
She kissed me goodnight
It was as cold as snow
She held me tight and close
The feeling she gives you
When you feel like letting go

Do Angels Cry?

Living life feeling dead inside is one Hell of a way to be alive
Lying up real late at night looking at the sky
I always wanted to know if angels cry

SECTION 5

Bury Me in a Bed of Roses

Bury me in a bed of roses
Thorns poking through my skin
Strange smells blowing in the wind
Memories of me fading into the abyss

The Beautiful Flower

The beautiful flower that lives today is dying tomorrow
Pulled out from the soil of fortitude
Held up in the highest light of adulation
The thorns of preservation dulled by molestation
The petals of vitality withering away into the abyss
The beautiful flower that once was yesterday shall be missed

If a Tree Falls

If a tree falls in the forest and nobody is around to hear it,
does it make a noise?

Let's be honest, nobody really cares.
Except for the rabbits, the birds and the bees.
And all the small animals that eat the leaves.
People got too much to be worrying about to be worried about some
trees.

The mighty tree in the forest finally came crashing down.
And when it hit the ground, nobody was even around.
Nobody knew the tree had fallen, because nobody heard the sound.
And when people finally stumbled upon the tree lying on the ground,
they just walked around.

The same tree that provided you with fruits, nuts, and seeds.
The same tree that provided you with the oxygen that you breathe.
The same tree that had its flesh carved in for the sake of love.
The same tree that provided you with shade when you went on a
hike or a walk.

The tree that stood the test of time.
The tree that faced nature in its prime.
The tree that helped the world be.
The tree that gave its all and never asked for anything in return.

The tree of life is dead now.

And nobody even heard a sound.

SECTION 6

Peace of Mind

My peace of mind
My peace of mind
I seek to find my peace of mind

Is it under a tree, or by a river, or in a cave
I can't seem to find my peace of mind

I call for help
But nobody seems to know which direction I should go

I have looked outward, I have looked within
Looking for my peace of mind has left my mind in pieces

Oh peace of mind
Oh peace of mind
Why are you so hard to find?

The Beaten Path

I thought I would take the road less traveled by
Turns out I went a little too far down
And got turned around
The good ole beaten path
Where dreams come to die

I Just Wanna Go To Sleep

I just wanna go to sleep
Late night my mind starts to creep
I think my dreams are better than reality
They want to know what's up with me
Open your eyes and then you will see
Nothing in this world is really what it seems

I just wanna go to sleep
I feel myself falling into the deep
Running from the things inside of me
Escape is never a guarantee
Locked in a lucid nightmare with no key

I just wanna go to sleep
Put my mind at ease
Letting go of this fallacy
A deep slumber I foresee
At rest is the only way I'll be free

You've Changed

I'm trying to keep the world from turning my heart cold

I can feel the ice forming in my veins

I'm smoking just to mask the pain

I'm standing in the eye of the storm

I'm dancing in the rain

They Want Hakuna Matata

They want hakuna matata
Steady drinking out the bottle
Trying to drown all their pain and their sorrow
Not even thinking about tomorrow

In the rain waiting for the sun to shine
Reminiscing on all the fun times
When everything felt just fine

Heart in a box and no key to unlock it
Wanna be free and fly high in the sky
Just like a pilot in a cockpit

Nothing is ever what it seems
Life is merely a dream
And everybody has to wake someday

SECTION 7

Death Knows Me Not

Death knows me not
He is not my friend
Cancer, falls, disease, war, and accidents
All the things that make a man meet his end

He who knows Death knows not
Death is immune to time
Pain, sorrow, grief, anger, and misery
All the things a man leaves behind

Death and I, we don't get along
But there will come a time
And it won't be long
'Till we're face to face

And only then
Will there be an end
to the life Death made me leave behind

My Homie Was A Soulja

My homie was a soulja
He was always prepared for battle
My homie was a soulja
He would never snitch or tattle

My homie was soulja
He always kept a weapon
My homie was a soulja
He was known for steppin'

My homie was a soulja
He never knew love
My homie was a soulja
He lived the life of a thug

My homie was a soulja
He was one of a kind
My homie was a soulja
He had a different state of mind

My homie was a soulja
He kept his people straight
My homie was a soulja
He made sure errybody ate

My homie was a soulja
He moved without a trace
My homie was a soulja
He looked death in the face

My homie was a soulja
He ain't never fold or bend
My homie was a soulja
He was solid 'til the end

My homie was a soulja
He gon rest in peace
My homie was a soulja
He gon live through me

Why'd you have to leave?

Why'd you have to leave?
I remember hanging out after school, you used to have to
sneak out the house just to chill. We started smoking weed,
you used to say you loved the way it made you feel. We came
from different backgrounds and different cultures but we
understood each other's struggles still. I had your back and
you had mine, you always kept it real.

Why'd you have to leave?
You were the reason people always felt included and
welcomed. You were the glue. You always made
everybody smile and laugh, no matter what you were
going through. And if there was a problem, I knew I could
always talk to you.

Why'd you have to leave?
I wish I could see your face one last time. I wish I could go
back in time and tell you what you meant to me. I wish
you could have seen the potential within yourself. I wish
you would have reached out and asked for some help. I
wish I would of noticed the signs. I wish what happened
didn't happen. I wish it was all a dream.

Tell me why'd you have to leave? Why'd you have to die?
I didn't even get a chance to say goodbye.

If We Are Going To Live

If we are going to live
Let us live like the kings and queens we are
Thriving and prosperous inside a paradise
Listening to the beautiful sounds of healthy and happy wildlife

If we are going to live
Let us live in a perpetual state of peace
Flourishing inside our precious kingdoms
Copiously existing with profuse and abundant sustenance

If we are going to live
Let us live with a purpose and a motive
Advantageously seizing every opportunity that this life gives
Maximizing the totality of our potential

If we are going to live
Let us live as if we were going to die tomorrow
Embracing and appreciating every moment
Enjoying everything that this world has to offer

SECTION 8

My love for you

If my love for you was a light
It would shine brighter than a thousand suns
The moon would be jealous of you
Because it is you who brightens my night

I want to swim in your love
But I get too scared when the water is deep
Your waves keep pulling me closer and closer
Your love is all I see
Tell me if I go under
Will you help me breathe?

The Creator of Love

When I was younger I didn't understand love
I thought it was a feeling that people experienced
But now I realize love isn't a feeling
It's an action
An action that shows itself through good times
An action that shows itself through difficult situations

Love is something you must constantly pursue
Anybody can have love
But you'll lose it if you're not willing to fight to keep it
Love as an action must be repeatedly expressed

I regret missing out on love
Waiting for the feeling
Waiting to see love
When love was waiting to be created
When love was a potential manifestation of a possible reality
I regret not noticing that I was the creator of love

Fear of Love

How do you want what you fear?
A fear of what you do not know
A desire for what you have never had

The dread of
The desire for

Love

She says that she loves me

She says that she loves me
But I think it's lust
I'm not saying that she's lying
But it's hard for me to trust

Scarred from past memories
Betrayal of the heart
I have to proceed with caution
I have to move smart

If I tell you I love you
Would you believe me
If I tell you I need you
Would you leave me

See me

Hear me

Feel me

Get to know the real me

She said she loved me

I said I loved her too

Who knew the love would fade

Who knew words spoken could be erased

Time heals all

But I can still see the wounds today

My pain from yesterday are the scars of tomorrow

Why didn't anybody tell me that love comes with sorrow

A Love Poem

Everybody wants to be a love poem
But most people don't know how to love
Would you know it if you saw it?
Or would you overlook it?

Too many people believe you have to pay for love
But then say love is priceless
Why treat love like a game?
Why is love all about what you can give and what the
other has to gain?

They ask me what my love languages are
I say all of them
I love with all my heart
I love with all my mind
I love with all my soul

But I'm picky
I don't share my love with everybody
I keep my love close
I know thieves will steal it in a heartbeat
And once it's gone, new love is hard to find
You might lose your soul and even your mind

What would you do for someone you love?
Would you lie?
Would you steal?
Would you die?
Would you kill?
What would you sacrifice for the sake of love?

What would you do for love?
If it fades would you let love go?
Or would you fight to keep it near?
The only thing scarier than love is the thought of fear

Nobody can teach you how to love
It's something you have to feel
Some people go their whole life not knowing if the love
they have is real

Some people question the meaning of life
Maybe love is the answer

What's life without love?
What's love without meaning?
The action is what makes love love
The expression of love shared

SECTION 9

She Was A Star

She was a star
Her energy was radiating
Her force pulled me in close
She shined even in her darkest hour
Her bright mind exuded exemplary excellence
Her magnetic personality was intrinsically captivating
She was always displaying an intensely exuberant vitality
Her warming essence was always of astronomical proportions
Her death leaving behind a black hole where my heart used to be
She had a scintillating presence that was of an immeasurable magnitude

Why is it that the largest stars always have the shortest lives?

She had a scintillating presence that was of an immeasurable magnitude
Her death leaving behind a black hole where my heart used to be
Her warming essence was always of astronomical proportions
She was always displaying an intensely exuberant vitality
Her magnetic personality was intrinsically captivating
Her bright mind exuded exemplary excellence
She shined even in her darkest hour
Her force pulled me in close
Her energy was radiating
She was a star

A letter to a past friend

Dear _____,

It's been a long time since we talked. And even though we were not around each other often or for long, I still remember the kindness you emitted whenever we were around each other. I still remember your smile which brought me comfort in a time in my life when genuine smiles were rarely given to me. Some people will never realize the impact they made on someone else.

If ever you feel overcome with darkness or despair, I hope you remember the radiating light inside of you, which has helped so many others out of their own darkness. I hope you never stop seeing the beauty in a world which can be so ugly. And I hope the beauty inside you remains as pure and intense as it was when I first met you.

Sincerely,

A friend from the past

Ain't Too Many

Ain't too many that can stand the rain
Ain't too many that can feel your pain
Ain't too many that can see your struggle
Ain't too many that can handle trouble
Ain't too many that will hold it down
Ain't too many that will stick around
Ain't too many that will keep it real
Ain't too many that will help you heal

ALL POWER TO THE PEOPLE

Violence Begets Violence

Violence begets violence
That's just how it goes
We see it in the movies
We hear it in the music
It's what the world knows
Violence is quick and fast
But peace comes slow
Can violence bring forth peace?
Or does violence cause the peace to go?
Some say peace is the absence of violence
Some would say no
Peace and violence
Like yin and yang
Both you must know
Peace is hard to get
Violence is hard to let go

What's Really Going On

They ask me if I know
I say I been knowing
They see it on the news
But I see it every day

What's really going on?

A couple billion to Ukraine
A couple billion to Israel
My grandma late on the rent still

In the Congo there's slavery
In Sudan there's war
Some junkie just overdosed in front of my auntie's door

You saw what happened in Haiti
You saw what happened in Palestine
Pookie got caught with some weed and the judge gave him hella time

There's concentration camps in China
There's women dying in Iran
A drive-by hit my cousin's house, the neighbors say it was a van

What's really going on?

They say no to reparations because they don't have the money
They say no to paying our student loans because they don't have the funds
Another war breaks out and they send a couple million dollars worth of guns

What's really going on?

I just hit the plug up to buy a couple banned books
I heard the food gives you cancer so I don't know what to cook

Another pipeline just leaked oil all over a native reservation
I heard my friend from high school was just shot outside a gas station

They just spent 200 billion dollars this year to keep people behind bars
I heard Elon and NASA just sent a couple rockets up to Mars

What's really going on?

I hope you know the diamonds in your chain are blood diamonds
I hope you know the cobalt in your phone is from child labor

I hope you know the likes on social media don't mean they like you for real
I hope you know the money will never make you feel how you want to feel

I hope you know this time here ain't forever
I hope you know there's always a bigger picture

I hope you know I been knowing
I hope you know now too

What's really going on

Young boy

In the soil is a young boy whose skin is like oil
Dirt all in his cuticles
Digging for gold and gemstones so you can look beautiful
Bodies missing
Diamonds glisten
Nobody listens
Just stroll on
Just scroll on
Don't worry about the cobalt that turns your phone on
Hurry hurry
In a scurry
It's not your problem
The world goes on
And on and on
Dusk and dawn
Faces drawn
Right and wrong
The world is torn
My oh my
Young boy
Young boy
Covered in mud
Covered in blood
Humanity dies every time another young boy is born
Begotten
Forgotten
Please don't let this world become rotten
Oh young boy

To see a bomb

Shooting stars up in the sky
I make a wish as they go by
I feel the tears coming from my eyes
Can the world hear us when we cry?

Shooting stars falling down
Dead bodies laying on the ground
Sad souls scattered all around
Do you know why children frown?

Shooting stars up in the sky
Shooting stars falling down
Will the world let us die?

I think I see a shooting star
I see the light up in the sky
The shooting star is not too far
Close my eyes and make a wish
I can hear the sound of a hiss

I open my eyes and look around
The shooting star is headed towards town
I try to change my wish but it's too late
The shooting star hits the ground
And seals my life's fate

Over And Over Again

Over and over and over again, they all do the same thang

Divide and conquer, there's a war on the brain

That's why I give them the words as drugs to stimulate their mainframe

But they miss the picture because it can't fit in the main frame

Oversized, I override the consciousness that resides inside

I manifest what tends to hide

Misaligned intentions began to synchronize

Creating a revolution that will never be televised

The Plight of A Patriot

All men are created equal
But you're a slave
We fight for freedom and sovereignty
But you better obey and behave
We made the rules, we set the standards
If you can't meet them then you're ill-mannered
The way you dress, the way you talk
Your hair, your skin, the way you walk
It's all wrong, it's just not right
What's that you say? You want rights
Don't you protest, you better not riot
Just go lay down and go be quiet
Don't come and march, don't take a knee
Why don't you just let things be?

They Do Kill

They do kill
They divide

They try to murder us, shoot us in the streets
Yet we are still alive
They try to starve us, give us nothing to eat
Yet we still survive

They do kill
They divide

They take us from our homes by force
They throw us in a cage
They say we are angry with no remorse
But they're the ones filled with rage

They do kill
They divide

They turn our friends into our enemies
They tell the world lies
They destroy all of our communities
They say we're playing victim when we cry

They do kill
They divide

They say the past is the past
But history is never ending
They say the nice guy finishes last
I guess that's why they're winning

They do kill
They divide

They see our numbers
But they skew the stats
We tried to trust them
But they stabbed our backs

They do kill
They divide

They tried to destroy us
Yet we stood tall
They tried to conquer us
Yet we did not fall

They do kill
They divide
They do kill
They divide

They do kill
But we don't die
They divide
But we multiply

SECTION 11

Imma Real Top Shotta

Imma real top shotta like Bob Marley
I shot the sheriff and went to war with the police
They don't protect us, they just serve us
And I'm justice hungry, I need more please

What I look like marching with my hands up yelling out don't shoot
Imma grab my staff like Moses and get to splitting until I see red seas
This one's for Fred, this one's for Huey, this one's for Bobby Hutton
You have to be willing to kill for something you love
Because it doesn't take much to die for nuthin'

A victim is someone who stands by and turns the other cheek
Like a pacifist
Even though you keep getting attacked with the pass of a fist
Imma step like David the slinger in Psalms 144
And speak blessing to the Lord for preparing my hands for war
No surrender, no retreat, death before defeat
I refuse to give up, I refuse to be beat
I refuse to live the rest of my life on my knees

I've been forced to hold the weight of this cold world on my head
And it's starting to make my brain freeze
So I have to fight back whether I win or whether I lose
I have to stand firm and remain solid, even during times of unease
Because a rock doesn't crumble to the strength of a breeze

Move Right Along

What I care 'bout a ban
I'm poled up
We got mo' guns than the Navy
Ain't seen this many ready for war since slavery
It'll behoove you to behave thee
Get to bucking and get to breaking
Ain't no I made thee
They gon have to grave me
Must be crazy

I only fear God not man
What I care 'bout a clan
Gon get rolled up
We got smoke for days
Right or wrong
Anybody can get got and gone
This here drill ain't no drill
We ain't singing no kumbaya song
So let the left alone be left alone and move right along

Sam I Am Not

I am not Sam
Sam I am not

I have no eggs
I have no ham
And all my milk has rot

Sam has plenty of food
But me, nothing is all I got
I envy Sam and his eggs and ham

Oh how I wish I could pick and choose
Whether it's red, green, or blue
But I have to eat whatever I can
Whether it comes in a bag, box, or can

If only I was as lucky as Sam
With an abundance of eggs and ham
But sadly, Sam I am not

PTSD

I think I saw a girl looking through my window
Am I paranoid or is somebody watching me
I hear a knock at my door
So I peek through the peephole
I see a group of guys with guns in their hands
And I think to myself
I don't know any of those people
So I act fast and grab my gun
Open the door and blast
Bullets flying around
All I hear is the sound of glass
I throw myself to the floor
Hit the ground quick and fast
It's an all out war and I might not last
I empty my magazine and I start to panic
I start running to my bedroom in a frantic
I slip and fall and hit my head
I'm thinking that they got me
I guess I'm dead
Loud sirens all around
I'm accepting my end now
I roll over and look up
And to my surprise
I couldn't believe my eyes

It was a clear blue sky
Suddenly the sound of sirens went away
And the group of guys were gone too
Just me sitting all alone in the middle of the street
With bruised hands and no shoes on my feet
Now that I think about it
I was nowhere near my house
And I don't even own a gun
I feel so confused
My thoughts are scrambled
I can't tell what's real and what's not
I'm at war

SECTION 12

Black Ole' Berry

All skin folk ain't kinfolk
Just because he's black don't mean he got my back
They say the blacker the berry the sweeter the juice
But some black berries are poisonous too
So you better be careful when you do what you do
Reconnecting with the roots
We a part of the same tree
But we don't all bear the same fruit

How can I be kind when the friend of my enemy is my kind
They say history repeats itself so let me rewind

They say the blacker the berry the sweeter the juice
Well I'm mad because I got a black ole' berry and it's a bitter fruit
Oh how sweet the smell is from the flower of the lie
But I can feel the pain from grabbing the thorn of truth
I just wish the juice from the berry of my reality was as sweet as the
fruit I produce

I'M BLACK

I'm black.

I'm black like Haiti in 1804.

I'm black like the Seminole War.

I'm black like Winnie Mandela and Assata Shakur.

I'm black like Sister Rosetta Tharpe with a guitar.

I'm black like the inventions of George Washington Carver.

I'm black like Huey P. Newton's peacock chair.

I'm black like the 1986 Olympics with black fists raised in the air.

I'm black like Ruby Bridges on her first day of school.

I'm black like Emmett Till lying in a casket.

I'm black like the money in Madam C.J. Walker's pocket.

I'm black like the Gullah Geechee speaking creole

I'm black like the Marcus Garvey play that inspired the Rastafari revolution.

I'm black like Yasuke in a foreign land with a katana in his hand.

I'm black like the Moors during Europe's dark ages.

I'm black like Malik Ambar leading an army of freed slaves in guerrilla warfare.

I'm black like the Dogon tribe talking about constellations.

I'm black like the Dahomey women warriors.

I'm black like the Africans that taught Pythagoras mathematics.

I'm black like the ancient Egyptians described by Herodotus.

I'm black like Imhotep practicing medicine.

I'm black like the land of Kemet where Plato, Thales, Aristotle, Euclid, and Socrates studied.

I'm black like Emperor Mansa Musa's brother, Abubakari before he sent a fleet of men to the Americas.

I'm black like the guanin gold tip spears that Christopher Columbus got from the Indigenous people.

I'm black like the locks that Delilah cut off from Samson's head.

I'm black like Moses when he was a baby in a basket sent down the river to be passed off as a child of the pharaoh, or when he performed a miracle and turned his hand white.

I'm black like negro spirituals being sung to the heavens by the harrowed souls of my ancestors.

I'm blacker than black.

I'm that black.

I'm blacker than History.

I'm blacker than the Future.

I'M BLACK!

I'm Not A Monster

They lock their doors as I walk by.
They clutch their purses as I say hi.
They stare at me with curiosity.
I approach them and they begin to flee.
What is wrong?
Why are you scared?
Is it me?
I feel the hate in their hearts.
I see the fear in their eyes.
Don't you know that I'm just a man?
I'm not a monster in disguise.

Descendant

I'm a descendent of the uncivilized tribes
The savages and the negros
Too unruly for a peace treaty
Too wild to assimilate
The bucks that couldn't be broken
The wool headed folk
The scarred skinned people
The scarry and dangerous ones

I'm a descendant of the ascended ones
The keepers of the sacred knowledge
The ones who breathe fire
The ones who dance rain
The ones who don't fear death
The ones who heal pain

I'm a descendant of the forgotten people
Fron the tribes said to be lost
From the people said to be crazy
From the ones said to be extinct

I'm a descendant of an ancient bloodline
A lineage from the spirt world

I'm a descendant of my ancestors

SECTION 13

Freedom Ain't Free

America is supposed to be the land of the free

But freedom ain't free, it cost a fee

Innocent or guilty, if you're poor you will still be copping a plea

And if you take it to trail, the judge will sentence you with a smile

Give you football numbers, have you gone for awhile

No money for bail?

Then I guess you're just going to be stuck in jail

No corrections, it's all about collections

How can one achieve sovereignty if you have to pay just to be?

Everybody is trying to figure out how to become free

Money is the key

Ballad Of An Inmate

Two noodles for a honeybun
Honeybun for a washcloth
I still don't have no soap tho
So I still can't wash off

They're banging on the walls
Everybody's screaming
So it's hard for me to think
Everybody's always hungry
We be drinking out the sink

The guards do the most
My cellie just died
He had an overdose

This hard mat hurts my back
There's mold on the walls
No money on my phone
Otherwise I would call

Everybody's at war
So in here it's kinda wild
Looking over my shoulder
It's been awhile since I smiled

They don't give us veggies
They don't give us fruits
No electronics
No books
There ain't shit for us to do

We ain't allowed to go outside
We barely get recreation
Only time we see a woman is at the nurses' station

Guards kicked me out the pod
I got into an altercation
They sent me to the hole
One month of segregation

Twenty-four hour lockdown
They won't even give us showers
The guards think it's funny
They keep abusing all their power
I can feel myself getting institutionalized
The new inmates can see it in my eyes
Incarceration only indignifies

Holidays going by
I'm counting down my time
I'm praying to the Lord
I'm trying to find peace of mind

What am I going to do when I get out
All the possibilities
All this time I've done has changed me
So what type of person am I going to be
When I finally get out
When I finally become free

I guess only time will tell
But until then
I'll be serving my time in hell

7.9.9.11

Tell me you see what I see
All the things this world has done to me

Made my heart so hard and cold
The good die young but the bad live old

Tell me why I try and fail
I look around and evil prevails

Trapped in a life that's a paradox
I am an open book inside a closed box

Tell me it's all one big illusion
That I'm a crazy outcast with delusion

In this wild world there is no escape
Destiny or coincidence, call it fate

Tell me that you see and feel my pain
Just like the sun when it can't shine through the rain

Oh freedom, you know you are not free
You have to die just to achieve sovereignty

Jack In The Box

Young Jack, he wants to be free but he's trapped in the box
If only Jack had a key or if he knew how to pick a lock

Every day was a struggle, he had to fight to survive
But he still made his prayers and he was thankful to be alive

Not knowing if he was ever going to be free or if he was there to rot
He never gave up hope, even if he did not have a lot

Head on a swivel, he can never be too careful
Stomach hurting and growling, in the box nobody is ever full

The box began to become his home
Always surrounded by people but yet he was still all alone

Abuse from the oppressor, abuse from the oppressed
Surrounded by violence, losing his peace to stress

Over time he began to change
Once a familiar face is now just something strange

Oh if they could only feel his pain they would understand
Life in the box is no place for a man

With no escape he began to accept his fate

If only he would have seen the exit before it was too late

With the conditions unbearable, he could not mask it

Out of the box, Jack went into the casket

SECTION 14

Who Dat Boy Is?

Who dat boy is?

"He walks around with his head held high"
"He must think he's better than us"
"He acts like he got it all figured out"
"He talks like he knows everything"

Who dat boy is?

"He thinks he's too good for this"
"He forgot where he comes from"
"He thinks he's one of them"

Who dat boy is?

"He act like he ain't scared of nothing"
"He ain't one of us"

Who dat boy is?

"He must think he's him"

Who dat boy is?

I Am That I Am

I keep trying to run from who I am
But I can't escape it
I am that I am
Like it
Loathe it
Hate it
Love it
I am that I am
I am the villain and the hero
I am the 1 and the 0
My fate is sealed with God
The wooden staff
The iron rod
Blessed through birth
Cursed with death
I am that I am
From the forsaken seed
From the begotten one
I am I
I am we
Of the all is all I am
I am that I am

I Reject Rejection

I'm walking barefoot on this lonely road covered in gravel
Oppression, depression, is it a blessing or a lesson
My confession is that I'm not obsessing over my impressions
I reject rejection
I am that I am with no objections
I could care less if you accept me

I Am Me

I am not my hair
  But my hair is me
I am not my skin
  But my skin is me
I am not the way I talk
  But the way I talk is me
I am not the way I dress
  But the way I dress is me
I am not where I'm from
  But where I'm from is me
I am not where I live
  But where I live is me
I am not who you perceive me to be
  I am me
I am not who you want me to be
  I am me

SECTION 15

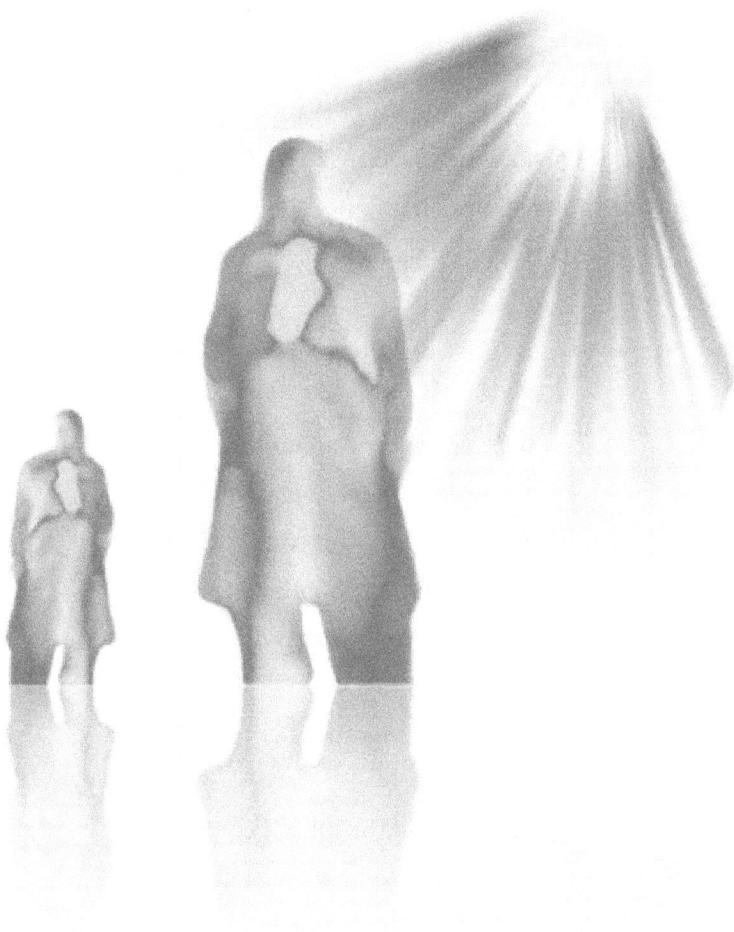

Sometimes I Cry

Sometimes I cry

I cry and I don't even know why
I guess it's just all the emotions I've bottled up over the years
Overflowing until there's nothing left but empty tears
Scars from past pains unseen by the naked eye

Sometimes I cry

I cry when reminiscing about how it used to be
Memories of what was
The regret of what could've been
Reconciling with the conflicts of my reality
No escape from the pains that lie within

Sometimes I cry

I cry for all the times I couldn't
When I had to be strong and brave
Fears faced
Demons conquered
Trials and tribulations
Decisions made

Sometimes I cry

I cry because sometimes that's all I can do
Limited outlets available
Riddled with emotions
Unable to shield my raw self

Sometimes I cry

With no other way for me to express my feelings
I let go just so I can hold on

I cry sometimes

Closed In

To my left
To my right
I'm surrounded

Am I the reason?
Is it because of something I did?
Or something I didn't do?

Feelings of claustrophobia creeping in
Too close for comfort

Should I try to fight it?
I don't think I will win
So what would be the point?
Maybe I should just accept it

All the things that led up to this
I don't see how this could of happened
It didn't use to be like this
Or maybe it did and I just didn't notice

Am I the only one?
Or is this happing to you too?
Maybe nobody else wanted to say anything
Or maybe I just didn't pay enough attention

I try to pretend that I'm ok with it
Some days I am
But most days it's too hard to handle

I smile and laugh
Maybe nobody will be able to tell
But deep down I will always know

I can't let anyone get too close
What if they start to see?
And once you see you can't unsee

Am I protecting them by staying away?
Or is that doing more harm than good?

I hope they know my intentions were pure
And that I meant well

If I let you in

If I let you in

You might see the pain I've hidden within

You might see the insecurities buried deep beneath the foundation

Watered down confidence in the soil of my imperfections

My self doubt taking root and starting to sprout into full-blown anxiety

My vulnerabilities blooming into depression

Hardened by my life experiences

My metamorphic transformation making me impenetrable to affection

My emotional aptitude hindered by underlying unaddressed traumas

My convoluted emotions forcing me into a paradoxical mental state of borderline hysteria

My covetous desire for companionship conflicting with my antisocial tendencies

Experiencing dissonance between my yearning for empathy and my apathetic thoughts

The tragedy of loss igniting my fear of new connections

The travesty of love fuming my insatiable appetite

I hope you realize that I'm a work in progress

A puzzle that is in the process of being solved knowing that there are a few pieces missing

I hope you realize that I tend to overthink and overanalyze

My past experiences making me skeptical and suspicious

Always contemplating and wondering about the ulterior motive

How can I begin to trust you when I can barely trust myself?

Always questioning the reason

How can I let you get to know me if I don't even know myself?

Always questioning whether it's real or not

How can I begin to love you when I'm struggling to love myself?

If I let you in

Do you promise not to be a visitor but a permanent resident?

One who can help me build

Walls structured with the reinforcement of communication

Windows sealed with the truth to keep lies from leaking in

Doors bolted with the compassion hinged on our understanding

I seek to listen to the burning desires from within

The inner essence of love waiting to be discovered

Will you accept me for me?

Through all my faults and downfalls

Will you accept me for me?

Through all the trials and tribulations

Will you accept me for me?

If I let you in

The Light Creates Shadows of My Darkness

The light creates shadows of my darkness
Being absorbed deep into my inner essence
Trying to protrude into the umbra of my soul
Only to be reflected back onto the source from which it came
Leaving me with an empty void yearning to be filled
A desire for an illuminating energy to feed my spirit
While I try to keep from descending into an entropic state of mind
Clinging onto my convoluted disintegrating sense of self
While I try to become one with the omnipresent consciousness
Hoping the entanglement of my emotions doesn't become conflated
with my actions

Even My Shadows

Even my shadows fear the darkness that lies within
Demons seeking refuge in the light
Angel wings draped in sin
Graven images on their walls
I see my reflection when I look at them
I call upon my inner spirit
Come and free me from myself

SECTION 16

The revenge of this world

You can't right your wrongs by doing wrong
You know two wrongs don't make a right
Getting revenge won't help you sleep better at night

You want to be a savior
But somebody should have told you
You risk losing yourself when you try to save the world

In the end all you have is yourself
And to save the world
You must first save yourself

So with that being said
Make sure you do right by yourself
And protect yourself from yourself

I hope you never forget
That in the end
The revenge of this world lies within

No Yes Men

Sometimes your best man is just a yes man
Until shit hits the fan
Then they get to second guessin'
Quick to question
Now they cursing your blessin's
So let this be a lesson
Never let someone hinder your progression
Even if a smile is what they expressin'
Sometimes their true intentions; they be suppressin'
Secretly praying for your possessions
Your downfall becoming their obsession

Endure The Struggle

Some people say there's beauty in the struggle
I say there's beauty in the ones that endure the struggle
The struggle that test morals and ethics
The struggle that builds resilience and fortitude
The struggle that develops compassion and character
The struggle that deepens understanding and empathy
To endure through trails and tribulations
To endure through suffering and hardships
The struggle of weathering the storm
That's what creates a beautiful radiating spirit

Unknown

I am not intimidated nor frightened by the unknown
Because I too am the unknown to whatever has yet to know me
I welcome the unknown
And hope to be embraced by whatever is unknown to me
I have become one with the unknown through my search to know
Yet I still battle between my desire to be known
And my desire to remain unknown

Note To Self

- Do better
- Manifest more
- Trust the process
- Be yourself
- Don't give up